Succession Management for Senior Military Positions

The Rumsfeld Model for Secretary of Defense Involvement

Andrew R. Hoehn, Albert A. Robbert, Margaret C. Harrell

RAND
CORPORATION

This publication results from the RAND Corporation's Investment in People and Ideas program. Support for this program is provided, in part, by the generosity of RAND's donors and by the fees earned on client-funded research.

Library of Congress Control Number: 2011927344

ISBN: 978-0-8330-5228-5

Published 2011 by the RAND Corporation
1776 Main Street, P.O. Box 2138, Santa Monica, CA 90407-2138
1200 South Hayes Street, Arlington, VA 22202-5050
4570 Fifth Avenue, Suite 600, Pittsburgh, PA 15213-2665
RAND URL: http://www.rand.org/
To order RAND documents or to obtain additional information, contact
Distribution Services: Telephone: (310) 451-7002;
Fax: (310) 451-6915; Email: order@rand.org

Preface

The selection of senior military officers for top-ranking positions is often a matter of speculation—Who among the military's three- and four-star ranks is to get what position or assignment?—but the process by which top leaders are selected is both rarely discussed and rarely the subject of analysis. This monograph aims to fill that gap by identifying recent practices used to select military officers for top-ranking positions and by identifying various criteria that should be considered by all future Department of Defense (DoD) leaders when establishing processes for selecting top leaders.

Our study began with the authors' interest in the officer selection process established by Donald H. Rumsfeld during his second tenure as Secretary of Defense. Rumsfeld came into the position determined to have an influence on the identification and selection of senior military officers for the top-ranking positions in DoD.[1] He believed that he had a mandate to transform the defense establishment and that institutions are transformed by the people responsible for leading them. He thus devoted considerable attention to creating a very different process for identifying and selecting senior military officers that drew heavily on input from his immediate civilian and military advisers but that offered a lesser role—or at least a different role—for the individual DoD military services, which, in the past, had had a preponderant

---

[1] Unless otherwise indicated, descriptions or quotations of personal opinions, thoughts, and beliefs reflect information reported to RAND Corporation researchers during interviews conducted in 2008, 2009, and 2010. Note that Rumsfeld was provided a draft of this manuscript.

influence on officer selection matters. He ultimately developed a process that featured long-term succession planning that looked beyond the next set of vacancies to be filled, built a slate of highly qualified officers, and sought to arrive at a series of "best fit" decisions for the top military positions across all the DoD services and joint commands. The process also focused on planning for the future—looking out some three to five years—by identifying highly capable leaders and associating them with a series of assignments that would prepare them for the top military positions.

Rumsfeld's changes to the officer selection process drew a range of reactions from the uniformed military community. Importantly, his changes also demonstrated that, to have staying power and produce consistent results, the process requires routine formal planning. He developed a process that looked across the talent produced by all the DoD military services and generated succession plans focused not just on the next round of senior officer changes but on two and even three changes into the future.

When Rumsfeld left DoD in 2006, parts of the process he developed were retained, and others were changed significantly or discarded. Since then, the process has continued to evolve, at times rekindling some of the efforts Rumsfeld initiated but reshaping them to suit the leadership style of current Secretary of Defense Robert Gates and the Chairmen of the Joint Chiefs of Staff who have served under him.

This monograph first examines senior leader selection and succession planning in general. It then focuses on the process developed by Rumsfeld and examines both how the process changed when Rumsfeld left DoD and how the process has evolved to date. This monograph does not offer conclusions about best practices but instead highlights the characteristics of various processes and offers suggestions about key system attributes that future DoD leaders should consider as they contemplate how senior officer selection and assignments will be managed.

This monograph should be of interest to current and future top DoD leaders—civilian and military—and those specializing in leader development and succession planning. The research was supported by RAND's Investment in People and Ideas program, which provides financial resources for independent, researcher-initiated inquiries, such as this one. However, the results presented here would not have been possible without the generous participation of a wide range of current and former top civilian and military leaders from DoD.

The principal investigator of this research is Andrew Hoehn. Comments are welcome and may be addressed to hoehn@rand.org.

Contents

Figures

Tables

Summary

Background and Introduction

The selection and assignment of the most senior military officers, those who wear three and four stars, include processes that, although well developed and long-standing, are generally unknown to most people, even those inside the armed forces. For many years, selection and assignment decisions were largely made within the services. Although the final decision fell to the Secretary of Defense, the Secretary typically did not challenge the recommendations of the services.

When Rumsfeld became Secretary of Defense in January 2001, he decided that he would become personally involved in the selection of officers for all three- and four-star assignments. Proponents of his involvement agreed with the need for his assertion of civilian control over the selection of officers who could help him transform DoD. Others viewed this change as an intrusion into processes that were best left to the Chairman of the Joint Chiefs of Staff and the military chiefs, who were more familiar with their own officers.

This monograph describes these processes and the context and perspectives that contributed to their development.

A Conceptual View

It is generally accepted that *succession planning* is practiced more robustly in the private sector than in the public sector. Not surprisingly, Rumsfeld and some of his key advisers (who, like Rumsfeld, had private-sector experience) found that the succession planning process they inherited for senior military leadership lacked some vital ingredients. Their experiences would likely have conditioned them to look for the following six elements:

- focusing on key positions
- identifying position-specific competency requirements and qualifications
- identifying and assessing high-potential candidates
- matching pools of candidates and positions, considering both near- and long-term successions
- using career paths to deepen and widen candidate pools
- engaging senior executives in the process.

As a seasoned executive, Rumsfeld had developed his own perspectives on succession management. In interviews with the authors, he identified the following as critical to succession planning:

- To maximize the chance of realizing an organizational vision, an executive needs people in key positions who share common goals.
- The recognition that people and positions change over time is important to putting the right people in the right positions.
- Executives must delegate many responsibilities, but succession management for senior subordinate positions is not one of them.
- A robust process is necessary to overcome the tendency to pick those you know for key positions, overlooking better, lesser-known candidates.
- The chief executive must pay attention to senior leader selection such that key subordinates will also pay more attention to it.

Some critics of Rumsfeld's active role in succession management viewed it as an unwarranted intrusion into the affairs of the Chairman of the Joint Chiefs of Staff (for joint positions) or the military chiefs (for service positions). However, we found that Rumsfeld's involvement was consistent with the principles of civilian control of the military as modified and clarified by the Goldwater-Nichols Defense Reorganization Act of 1986 and with statutory provisions (10 U.S.C. 601) pertaining to appointments to fill three- and four-star positions.

The Historical Context

When Rumsfeld began his second tenure as Secretary of Defense, he perceived several fundamental problems with the processes used to choose senior military leaders to be recommended for higher rank or additional assignments. First, he perceived a lack of explicit criteria for each position that should guide the selection of the most appropriate candidate. Second, he found that, although each service was required by law to submit at least one nominee for joint four-star vacancies, the services were not consistently offering viable candidates. Instead, the services appeared to be submitting strong candidates only when they perceived that it was their "turn" to fill a position in an understood pattern of job rotations or when the position had traditionally been filled by the service. Rumsfeld found the lack of both explicit criteria and a truly competitive process for filling the most senior military positions to be in conflict with his management philosophy. He also felt it important to challenge the services to provide the very best candidates for all three- and four-star assignments.

There are several key aspects of the process that Rumsfeld introduced. First, the decisions involved four key decisionmaking members: the Secretary of Defense, the Deputy Secretary of Defense, the Chairman of the Joint Chiefs of Staff, and the Vice Chairman of the Joint Chiefs of Staff. Although the final decision belonged to the Secretary of Defense, all accounts suggest that the discussions held by this group, which became known informally as the personnel committee, did inform—and sometimes change—the final decision. It is important to note that the military chiefs were not included in this small group of decisionmakers.

These decisionmakers, including Rumsfeld, personally interviewed candidates as part of the evaluation and decision process. In addition to interviewing candidates for specific assignments, Rumsfeld also sought to interview high-potential officers whenever he was traveling to their locations or otherwise had the opportunity to do so.

Rumsfeld noted early in his second tenure as Secretary of Defense the lack of explicit, position-specific criteria for selection. The personnel committee and its supporting staff developed these criteria and adopted associated evaluation tools in the form of matrixes used to rate the competencies and qualifications of various candidates. Another important tool was "the Board," a felt-covered piece of plywood with the names of various positions and candidates attached by a Velcro-like material. This tool permitted the personnel committee to consider current and future vacancies in their entirety.

The process that emerged under Rumsfeld included both *slating* and *laydowns*. Slating addressed near-term vacancies. It differed from the prior, conventional practice in that multiple vacancies were considered simultaneously rather than sequentially. The Board facilitated this process by allowing the decisionmakers to explore alternatives by moving positions and candidates to various places on the felt surface. Laydowns—a relatively new concept for most of the military services—entailed the purposeful identification and development of high-potential officers for future assignments, and they were discussed once or twice a year during private sessions between a service chief and Rumsfeld. These laydown discussions would sometimes cover, for example, the career paths recommended for high-potential one- and two-star officers to prepare them for specific three- and four-star assignments.

Another important aspect of the Rumsfeld process was the prioritization of assignments. Contrary to traditional military culture, which had prioritized the service chief as the preeminent assignment, Rumsfeld made the combatant commander positions the most important. He also placed a new emphasis on joint deputy commander positions, considering them to be developmental opportunities rather than career pinnacles.

The Process

Prior to the changes introduced by Rumsfeld and his advisers, the central role in the selection of officers for senior joint positions was played by the Chairman of the Joint Chiefs of Staff. As shown in Figure S.1, the process was linear and sequential: Typically, each vacancy was con-

Figure S.1
The Prior Process for Senior Joint Position Nominations

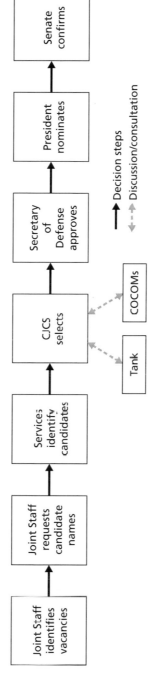

NOTES: CJCS = Chairman of the Joint Chiefs of Staff. COCOM = combatant commander.

sidered and filled with little or no regard for other vacancies that might arise at other times.

Rumsfeld's process, when fully implemented, had the elements depicted in Figure S.2. The central role was played by the personnel committee, with supporting participation provided by one or more special assistants. Key elements included service laydowns, consideration of multiple candidates for multiple positions, consideration of candidates for key service and joint positions, and the potential for Rumsfeld and his staff to identify candidates beyond those recommended by the military chiefs.

Immediately following Rumsfeld's departure in 2006, the process largely reverted to a linear form similar to that which prevailed prior to his arrival in 2001. Some elements, such as service laydowns and the review of candidates by the similarly constituted personnel committee, were retained, at least initially. However, as shown in Figure S.3, primary responsibility for the process shifted to the Chairman of the Joint Chiefs of Staff.

Figure S.2
The Rumsfeld Process

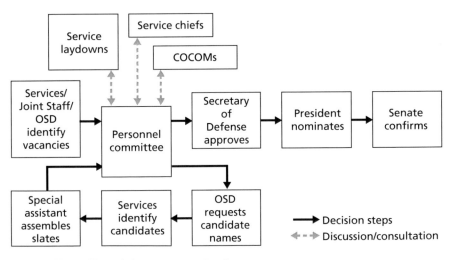

NOTE: OSD = Office of the Secretary of Defense.
RAND *MG1081-S.2*

Figure S.3
The Post-Rumsfeld Process for Senior Joint Position Nominations

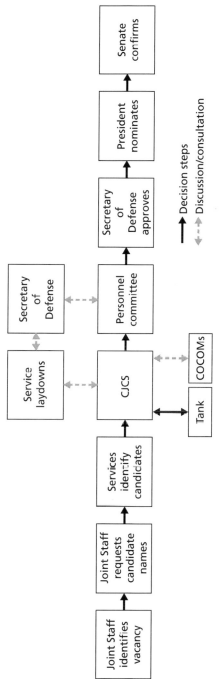

RAND *MG1081-S.3*

Returning to the six important elements of a succession planning process, identified earlier, we evaluated the Rumsfeld process and the prior and subsequent processes. Our assessments are shown in Table S.1, where a black checkmark indicates a robust implementation and a gray checkmark indicates a more limited implementation. The absence of a checkmark indicates that the element was or is not a consistent feature of the process.

Overall, we found that the Rumsfeld process, as it finally evolved, contained most of the expected elements of a fully formed succession management system. However, in the view of some key stakeholders (mainly, some military chiefs), there were unresolved issues: lack of transparency in personnel committee deliberations, poor understanding of the role of the special assistant who managed the process for the Secretary, and discomfort with the laydown process.

Table S.1
Assessing the Processes

	Prior Process	Rumsfeld Process	Subsequent Process
Focus on key positions	✓	✓	✓
Identify position-specific competency requirements and qualifications		✓	
Identify and assess high-potential candidates	✓	✓	✓
Match pools of candidates and positions, considering both near- and long-term successions		✓	✓
Use career paths to deepen and widen candidate pools		✓	✓
Engage senior executives in the process	✓	✓	✓

Conclusions and Recommendations

The two most important elements introduced by Rumsfeld and his personnel committee were (1) the active, engaged participation of the Secretary of Defense in the selection of officers for senior positions and (2) the identification and development of high-potential, more junior officers. Another key contribution was the simultaneous consideration of multiple candidates and multiple vacancies, which was intended to optimize the selection process. These elements appear to have been significantly deemphasized after Rumsfeld's departure. Much of the deliberation undertaken in selecting candidates for joint positions moved from the personnel committee to the Joint Chiefs of Staff tank, and the selection of officers to fill positions within the services was left largely to the military chiefs and secretaries.

We propose the following recommendations for future processes:

- Consider establishing a senior general/flag officer management office (GOMO) within the Office of the Secretary of Defense, with its chief reporting directly to the Secretary of Defense, to provide staff support for joint succession planning. (See p. 52 for special requirements related to the position.)
- Require the senior GOMO to develop tools and information systems to support simultaneous consideration of multiple candidates for multiple positions.
- Require the senior GOMO to maintain descriptions of the qualifications and expertise required for senior positions.
- Clarify the purpose and desired content of service laydowns, focusing them specifically on longer-term personnel plans.
- The Secretary and Deputy Secretary of Defense should be closely involved in the selection of senior leaders and should understand the strengths and weaknesses of each selected officer as well as the characteristics of the officers not selected for each position.
- The Secretary of Defense, with the participation of the personnel committee, should explicitly prioritize senior leader positions and ensure that the best candidates are selected for the highest-priority positions.

Acknowledgments

This research would not have been possible without support and cooperation from numerous individuals. We thank Donald H. Rumsfeld for his receptiveness to our research inquiry and for encouraging DoD leaders who were involved in the process to speak with us openly and candidly. We also want to thank General James Cartwright, Admiral Vernon Clark, General John Craddock, Rudy DeLeon, Raymond Dubois, Gordon England, General William Fraser, Admiral Edmund Giambastiani, General Michael Hagee, Lernes Hebert, Stephen Herbits, Vice Admiral Staser Holcomb, General John Jumper, Kenneth Krieg, Admiral Michael Mullen, Colonel Conrad Munster, General Richard Myers, General Peter Pace, General Joseph Ralston, General Peter Schoomaker, General Norton Schwartz, General Walter Sharp, Cecile St. Julien, and Paul Wolfowitz. We are especially grateful to Stephen Herbits and Staser Holcomb for providing comments on earlier drafts. This monograph has also been improved by the peer reviews of RAND colleague William M. Hix and by an external reviewer. We appreciate their constructive suggestions.

We are grateful to James Thomson and Michael Rich of RAND, who encouraged us to pursue our interest in this topic, and to Richard Neu, who facilitated this opportunity within RAND.

Abbreviations

CJCS	Chairman of the Joint Chiefs of Staff
COCOM	combatant commander
DoD	Department of Defense
GOMO	general/flag officer management
OSD	Office of the Secretary of Defense
VADM	vice admiral

CHAPTER ONE

Introduction

Background

Each of the four Department of Defense (DoD) military services has generally well-developed processes for developing officers for service positions. These processes involve varying periods of service in line and staff positions interspersed with intensive periods of training and education. Following the landmark Goldwater-Nichols Defense Reorganization Act of 1986, the military services were required to reassess their processes for selecting officers to serve in "joint" as well as single-service positions. Indeed, the accumulation of joint duty experience took on such importance that it became a prerequisite for promotion to more senior military ranks.

The process of evaluating and selecting officers for the most senior positions (i.e., the three- and four-star ranks) stands in contrast to the very elaborate processes used to develop and select officers for lower ranks. Individual services typically recommend officers for various senior positions (both individual service and joint positions), and these recommended officers are reviewed by the Secretary of Defense or his designees. The Secretary subsequently recommends the candidate officer to the President for presidential nomination and subsequent congressional confirmation. Although much has been said about the individuals ultimately selected for senior positions, relatively little is known or has been written about how this selection process takes place.[1] Earlier

---

[1] On occasion, such as when a senior officer was disqualified for a particular position, the process would become somewhat more transparent. Typically, however, far more attention has been paid to who was chosen rather than who did the choosing or how it was done.

selection processes may have been effective—clearly, scores of exceptional officers have served in the top military positions—but it is not clear whether they were influenced more by the military services that nominated individuals for particular positions or by the DoD civilian leadership that oversaw and ultimately selected the candidates.

Upon becoming Secretary of Defense in January 2001, Donald H. Rumsfeld decided he would be personally involved in the selection of all three- and four-star military officers, and he established a detailed screening and selection process for all senior military positions.[2] The process drew upon traditional service nominations,[3] but it added a more thorough screening and interview process that involved the Secretary of Defense, the Deputy Secretary of Defense, the Chairman of the Joint Chiefs of Staff, and the Vice Chairman of the Joint Chiefs of Staff. The process was organized by a special assistant to the Secretary, who screened the service nominees, developed a tentative slate of candidates, and helped arrange for the candidates to meet individually with the four leaders involved in the selection process. Once the interviews were complete, the leaders met to discuss the candidates. They considered a wide array of factors but focused particularly on the candidates' joint qualifications, even in the cases of those considered for senior positions within the military services. On most occasions, the Secretary of Defense then selected nominees from the list of available candidates; on a few occasions, after conferring with his top advisers, he reopened the selection process to seek a wider set of candidates.

Some saw this new process as an intrusion of the Secretary of Defense into the officer selection process; others applauded the effort, calling it a welcome move in the direction of greater civilian

---

[2]   Unless otherwise indicated, descriptions or quotations of personal opinions, thoughts, and beliefs reflect information reported to RAND Corporation researchers during interviews conducted in 2008, 2009, and 2010. Note that Rumsfeld was provided a draft of this manuscript.

[3]   Each of the four DoD military services traditionally nominates officers for senior military positions.

control of the military.[4] However, no one other than the immediate decisionmakers appears to have been granted visibility into

- how the selection process was organized
- who was involved in screening and selecting candidates
- how nominations were brought forward by the military services
- what criteria were used in choosing candidates
- how nominations ultimately were presented to the Congress for confirmation by the Senate.

This monograph seeks both to document the process that was established by Rumsfeld during his second tenure as Secretary to select the nation's top military leaders and to compare it with the preceding process and the processes that have evolved since his departure. This monograph focuses in particular on succession planning as a theme and on how the various approaches adopted by recent DoD leaders have sought to align the best talent available against an array of highly demanding leadership positions.

What distinguishes the process that Rumsfeld developed was the intense personal involvement it required of the Secretary of Defense. As discussed later in this monograph, this high level of personal involvement is consistent with what the management literature would lead one to expect of top-performing leaders. But it did not come without a cost. Some viewed the process as intrusive and meddlesome, as interfering with the traditional prerogatives of the military chiefs and ultimately undermining the judgment of the nation's top military leadership. Others, however, came to view it as one of Rumsfeld's key accomplishments as Secretary of Defense. Some closest to the process viewed Rumsfeld's involvement not as interfering with the military chiefs' prerogatives but as denying the chiefs the ability to play favorites without regard to the broader needs of the defense establishment or the public interest as a whole.

---

[4] Our brief examination of the debate at the time suggests that neither detractors nor supporters considered the role of the Chairman and Vice Chairman of the Joint Chiefs of Staff in the process.

The officer selection process that Rumsfeld developed during his tenure did not survive his departure. Soon after being confirmed as Secretary of Defense, Robert Gates agreed to assign many of the duties of selecting the top military leaders to the Joint Chiefs of Staff. He decided that he would review and approve their recommendations but would not be heavily involved in the selection process. The process that evolved after Rumsfeld's departure focused less on succession planning and more on filling immediate vacancies. Over time, however, Gates and the current Chairman of the Joint Chiefs of Staff, Admiral Michael Mullen, have become more involved in the day-to-day matters of picking the nation's top military leaders and have attempted to reintroduce the idea of succession planning or, as one observer put it, "looking out two or more moves as we choose today's leaders."

Approach

Most of our findings are based on a series of RAND interviews with the principals and key stakeholders engaged in the process of managing senior officer selections before, during, and after Rumsfeld's second tenure as Secretary of Defense. Interviewees included Rumsfeld himself; his special assistant, VADM Staser Holcomb (U.S. Navy, Retired), who organized and managed the process for Rumsfeld; and Stephen Herbits, who originally developed several of the ideas that would later come to characterize the Rumsfeld process. Others included current or former Deputy Secretaries of Defense, Chairmen and Vice Chairmen of the Joint Chiefs of Staff, military chiefs, military assistants to the Secretary of Defense, and Directors of the Joint Staff. Many of those interviewed had also served as commanders of major service commands or joint combatant commands and therefore provided perspective from those positions as well.

The three authors of this monograph participated in most of the interviews. We developed a semi-structured protocol with a standard list of questions that were asked in each of the interviews. We supplemented these questions with others, depending on the position of the person during his time of service and his role in the various processes.

Some interviewees served during times that preceded Rumsfeld's era, some during his tenure, and some after. We encouraged frank discussions during the interviews by agreeing not to record individuals' names in our notes and by agreeing to focus primarily on the overall process, selection criteria, and results rather than on the process as it pertained to outcomes for third parties (e.g., why person X was selected for job Y). However, when the names of specific individuals have been reported in other published works in connection with particular statements or activities, we may report them here. Although we conducted the interviews on the record, we also offered individuals the opportunity to provide comments that would not be attributed to them. Even in these instances, however, we acknowledged that some comments might be attributable to individuals by inference.

We were given access to records that supplemented our interviews. Our goal in searching through these records was not to determine who was or was not selected for a given position but rather both to document the process that was developed to select the nation's top military leadership and to determine the criteria used to make those selections. We draw upon some of this material in the remainder of this monograph.

We supplemented our interviews with a review of the literature on succession management and, in the case of two of the authors, with extensive professional expertise in the field of personnel development and management. We used this literature review and each author's prior research on the management of senior military officers as the basis for postulating the elements we would expect to see in a robust succession management system for senior military positions in DoD. We used this framework to evaluate the processes described to us during interviews.

Organization of This Monograph

This monograph begins with a general examination of succession planning as understood in the management literature and then looks in detail at senior officer selection processes within DoD. Chapter Two provides a conceptual view of succession management. It outlines the elements found in robust succession management systems, summarizes Rumsfeld's personal perspectives on the senior officer selection process as they were described to us, and identifies the constitutional principles and statutory requirements that are unique to the selection process in the case of senior military leaders. Chapter Three describes how the process evolved during Rumsfeld's second tenure as Secretary of Defense and how some of the key decisions he faced during that time influenced the evolution of the process. In Chapter Four, we compare and assess three approaches to succession management—the process prior to Rumsfeld's tenure, the fully evolved process that he and his key advisers developed, and the process as that evolved after his departure. Chapter Five presents our conclusions and recommendations.

CHAPTER TWO

A Conceptual View

In contemporary human resource management practice, the recruiting, selection, development, and utilization of senior executives is understood to require special attention. Leaders are given authority and responsibility to guide their organizations toward desired outcomes. Their effects vary, depending on how well suited they are to their organizations and their challenges. Accordingly, a systematic approach to identifying and developing leaders is an important element of organizational success.

Succession planning and *succession management* are terms commonly used to describe this systematic approach (Huang, 2001; Jarrell and Pewitt, 2007; Lynn, 2008). Succession planning and succession management processes commonly contain elements of both *development* and *utilization*. Developmental elements focus on identifying future human capital needs; identifying individuals with high potential to meet those needs; and investing appropriately in the training, education, and experience of high-potential candidates. Utilization processes focus on matching the available talent and the immediate needs of the organization.

Private-sector implementation of succession management is generally regarded as more robust than that found in the public sector (Fulmer and Conger, 2004; Hardy, 2004–2005; Lynn, 2008; NAPA, 1997). Hardy (2004, p. 42) attributes this in part to the difficulties presented by an environment in which preselection for development purposes may be considered a violation of equal employment opportunity laws.[1]

Not surprisingly, when Rumsfeld left a chief executive officer position in the private sector to enter his second tenure as Secretary of Defense, he was eager to address succession planning for senior military leadership in DoD. He felt that the DoD system lacked some vital ingredients to which he, and some of his key advisers who also had private-sector experience, had become accustomed.[2] For example, the process focused on near-term assignments—i.e., on who gets the next job—but not on long-term career development that considers the best talent across all four DoD services. Assignments often took place on a rotating schedule that gave the military services "turns" placing their top talent into specific positions, whether or not the person selected was the best fit for the position. This custom afforded each service a fair share of the top military positions. Rumsfeld and his advisers were also acutely aware that advancement within the military services takes place within a closed system: Those being promoted to the top ranks had entered military service some 30 years earlier, and the military personnel system does not allow for lateral entry, which would refresh the ranks. As a result, they were intent on bringing an outsider's view to the process.

In this chapter, we summarize the key elements of succession management as they apply in the case of senior military officers. We also provide some of Rumsfeld's personal perspectives on the process. Finally, we describe the constitutional and legal mandates that establish some of the structure within which succession management must occur.

---

[1] It is not uncommon for the military services to identify high-potential officers early in their careers and to track those officers throughout their time in service. The successful performance of these officers is often reflected in early promotion to more senior ranks and in these individuals being considered for more-favorable assignments. These assignments often lead to promotion to even more senior ranks.

[2] Most notable among these was Herbits, a special assistant to the Secretary during the earlier part of Rumsfeld's term.

Elements of Succession Management

Distilling various practices found in both public- and private-sector succession management, we identified six elements that we believe are especially important in fostering effective senior joint leadership. In this section, we describe each of those elements and our rationale for including them.[3]

Engaging Senior Executives in the Process

Senior executives, and in particular the chief executive of an organization, are expected to set a vision for the direction of the organization. Implementing the chief executive's vision requires the cooperation of like-minded and competent executives at lower levels. Accordingly, an effective chief executive with strong interest in implementing a vision will also have a strong interest in finding, developing, and placing the right people in key subordinate executive positions. The chief executive's role, in which he or she is assisted by other key senior executives, is to link succession management to organizational strategy. In DoD, the chief executive is the Secretary of Defense. Key subordinates include the Deputy Secretary of Defense, the Chairman of the Joint Chiefs of Staff, the Vice Chairman of the Joint Chiefs of Staff, and the service secretaries and chiefs. Over time, all have played various roles in selecting leaders to fill specific vacancies and in managing the overall succession process—to the extent that a succession planning process existed. Often, however, DoD's chief executive (i.e., the Secretary of Defense) has delegated many of the responsibilities for filling vacancies to the uniformed military leadership.

The military services have a history of strong leadership involvement in their internal succession processes, although that involvement

---

[3] Some elements commonly found in succession management processes were not included in our analysis because they have little or no applicability in this context. These include performance management and formal feedback systems (which are managed by the services rather than the Office of the Secretary of Defense [OSD]), compensation (which is strictly tied to grade for general/flag officers), retention (there is no statutory authority to provide retention incentives at the general/flag officer level), external recruiting (which is not applicable in closed personnel systems), and workforce planning (which is managed by the services rather than OSD).

is generally much more extensive on the part of what might be regarded as the chief operating officer (the service chief) rather than the chief executive officer (the service secretary). That involvement is evidenced by the periodic requests RAND has received from military chiefs for advice or assistance regarding their processes. However, there is little evidence that, before Rumsfeld's second tenure as Secretary of Defense, a formal succession planning process existed in DoD outside beyond that which exists in the military services, which traditionally plan to fulfill service needs (e.g., what is best for the Army, Navy, Air Force, or Marine Corps) rather than DoD needs. The services do seek to place their general/flag officers in strategically important joint positions but are not responsible for determining total joint leadership needs or ensuring that those needs are met through appropriate development of sufficient numbers and kinds of officers. Indeed, prior to enactment of the Goldwater-Nichols reforms, joint experience (e.g., experience in OSD, the Joint Staff, the combatant commands, and the defense agencies) was neither formally tracked nor a requirement for promotion to more senior military ranks.

Focusing on Key Positions

Organizational effectiveness depends more critically on some positions than on others. Positions that are higher in the organizational hierarchy and more closely aligned with the core business of the organization tend to have greater strategic impact. Because senior executive attention is a scarce resource, a top-level succession management process must be focused on the positions that matter the most. In DoD, where warfighting ultimately is the core business, leadership in the combatant commands and the Joint Staff is most critical, but leadership within the military services, which have an organize, train, and equip function, is also important in achieving an overall strategic vision for national defense. Historically, filling important military service positions has received the preponderant share of attention; positions within the combatant commands (especially key staff positions) and, until recently, the Joint Staff have received less attention. For example, each of the combatant commands has a large supporting staff with hundreds of positions filled by flag/general officers, field-grade officers, senior noncommissioned officers, and civilians. With a few exceptions—including the Joint Staff—assignment to these staffs tends not to be as carefully managed as assignment to the military service staffs.[4]

Identifying Position-Specific Competency Requirements and Qualifications

In an empirical study of the elements of successful leadership succession, Gabarro (1987, p. 68) observed that "the all-purpose general manager who can be slotted into just about any organization, function, or industry exists only in management textbooks." His findings underscore the need to tailor development and utilization to the specific needs of various positions. Matching people and positions or preparing individuals for future positions is much more likely to proceed systematically if everyone involved in the process has a common understanding of the competencies, experiences, temperament, and other characteristics considered conducive to success in a given position at a given time. Common understanding is reached by making the requirements explicit.

For example, within DoD, the requirements placed on the various combatant commands, and, therefore, the responsibilities of the commander and his staff, tend to change over time. U.S. European Command offers a good illustration of this phenomenon. U.S. European Command was once considered the key warfighting command in the U.S. command structure. Those assigned to U.S. European Command and its key subordinate organizations (e.g., U.S. Army Europe, U.S. Air Forces Europe) would presumably have been screened for their warfighting credentials. Those assigned to other warfighting commands understood that, if there were a war in Europe, their responsibility was to support the activities of U.S. European Command. That, of course, is no longer the case. U.S. European Command remains a

---

[4]   Further, before Rumsfeld's second tenure as Secretary, assignment to Joint Staff positions was generally not held in as high esteem as assignment to service staff positions, as became evident in the need for the Goldwater-Nichols Defense Reorganization Act to legislate that officers serving in these positions (as well as Joint Specialty Officers) must be selected for promotion (including to the ranks of O-7 and O-8) at rates commensurate with officers serving in service staff positions.

highly important command, given the relationships the United States has with its European partners, but it is no longer viewed as a key warfighting command or, for that matter, as a key command to be supported by other commands. In fact, in early 2003, during preparations for war with Iraq, a banner hung in U.S. European Command headquarters in Stuttgart, Germany, asked, "What have we done lately to support Central Command?" The banner was referring, of course, to U.S. Central Command, which has responsibilities for large portions of the Greater Middle East. This change in emphasis for U.S. European command would, should, and did have an effect on judgments about the type of leadership assigned to the command.

Identifying and Assessing High-Potential Candidates

Development and utilization decisions depend not only on position requirements but on knowing who the high-potential candidates are, how well their characteristics match the demands of various positions, and how gaps in their preparation can be closed.

McCall (1998, pp. 146–153) describes how these elements come together in organizations that practice systematic succession planning. He advocates maintaining two lists of potential replacements for key assignments: A-list candidates ready for the job and B-list candidates who have high potential but lack some critical experience. He further advocates assessing not only the performance demands of key assignments but also what the assignments might teach their incumbents. When a vacancy occurs, decisionmakers must weigh the need for near-term performance (implying selection from the A list) relative to the need to develop talent for longer-term performance (implying selection from the B list). A systematic approach such as this demands that much about both job and individual characteristics is made explicit.

Within the military services, such ranking clearly exists. This becomes apparent when senior officers are placed in development roles or are "parked" until future opportunities arise. We are not aware of any such ranking or list across service leadership talent that addresses the development of officers for joint opportunities.

Matching Pools of Candidates and Positions

Near-term organizational interests can be optimized by putting the best available candidate in a vacant position. A longer view may suggest a different strategy. First, the best candidate for the immediate vacancy may also be the best candidate for a more critical position that will become vacant later. Second, as mentioned earlier, longer-range considerations may lead organizations to fill a vacancy with an individual who is less qualified than other available candidates but more in need of the experience the position will impart. McCall, Lombardo, and Morrison (1989, p. 2) argue that the bulk of executive development takes place on the job rather than in the classroom. Thus, using positions to develop executive talent introduces a tension between near- and long-term needs that demands thoughtful consideration.

For example, the best candidate for the position of deputy commander of one of the regional combatant commands may be an individual with deep experience in the region, particularly someone with prior service within the command. But, from a developmental standpoint, it might be more important to assign the deputy role to a highly talented officer who could both learn by observing the commander and participate in the decisionmaking process, whether or not that officer has any particular experience in the geographic area. In this sense, the deputy might be being groomed for a more senior position in a subsequent assignment.[5]

Similarly, Graham (2009) relates, Rumsfeld and his advisers had decided to assign a senior Army general to command the newly established U.S. Northern Command, which has responsibility for the defense of North America. The Army general had accumulated considerable experience in the joint arena and would have been ideal as head of the new command. But Rumsfeld and his advisers were also looking to choose a successor for the Army Chief of Staff in the not-too-distant future, so, upon reflection, they deferred appointing the Army general

---

[5] Rumsfeld was particularly interested in getting more value from the deputy positions in the combatant commands. Rather than seeing these positions as end-of-career assignments for solid leaders who would not likely reach four-star rank, he saw these positions as grooming areas that should be used to prepare highly qualified officers for subsequent, more senior assignments.

to head the new command and instead chose to recommend him as Army Chief of Staff.[6]

Using Career Paths to Deepen and Widen Candidate Pools

This element is closely related to the previous one. When, for development purposes, an individual is deliberately placed in a position for which there were better-qualified candidates, the placement will best benefit the organization if it is part of a carefully considered career path. Morrison and Hock (1986, p. 237) define a career as "a sequence of work roles that are related to each other in a rational way so that some of the knowledge and experience acquired in one role is used in the next." Harrell et al. (2004) discuss this phenomenon in a military context, indicating that patterns of development toward very senior positions continue even after promotion into the general/flag officer ranks. For example, the services recognize the value of having officers with operational experience occupy senior positions in weapon system acquisition programs. However, in addition to operational experience, these positions often require certification of specific acquisition-related experience.[7] Providing the requisite acquisition experience to officers with operational backgrounds while at the same time preserving their operational competencies requires a careful rotation between operational and acquisition duties. Although these officers, during their initial assignments in acquisition roles, may perform less competently in program management positions than officers whose full careers have been in acquisition assignments, the alternative is a loss of opportunity to introduce operational perspectives at the senior program management level.

---

[6] See Graham, 2009. It is worth noting that General Jack Keane, who was selected to become Army Chief of Staff, did not ultimately serve in the position.

[7] 10 U.S.C. 433 specifies that

> [t]he head of each executive agency shall ensure that appropriate career paths for personnel who desire to pursue careers in acquisition are identified in terms of the education, training, experience, and assignments necessary for career progression to the most senior acquisition positions.

Opportunities for development through job rotations are, of course, limited by the number and development potential of available positions. Thus, in succession management, it is advantageous to chart the proposed career paths of multiple candidates simultaneously, using considerations that will optimally develop the pool of candidates for future critical positions.

Rumsfeld's Perspectives

As a seasoned executive, Rumsfeld had developed many of his own perspectives on succession management. His long history of government and private-sector experience reinforced his view that choosing capable leaders is perhaps one of the two most important functions of a senior executive; the other, of course, is to set overall direction for the activities of the organization. During Rumsfeld's first appointment as Secretary of Defense (1975–1977), he became concerned that senior officer promotions and assignments reflected a certain cronyism among the military services and that top leaders were chosen because they were former academy classmates or roommates of serving officials. He was also concerned that if highly capable leaders had not been given opportunity to have the "right" experiences and assignments, they would not be considered qualified for the most senior positions. Finally, he worried that there may have been too much of a gentleman's agreement among the military chiefs regarding who would receive the top assignments and that this came at the expense of an open process that allowed the best talent to compete for assignments over time. During his second tenure as Secretary of Defense, Rumsfeld felt it important that he attend to some of these concerns. He was eager to apply what he learned from his earlier government and corporate experiences to the challenge of choosing the nation's top military leadership.

During interviews, Rumsfeld particularly focused on the five features described in the subsections that follow.

Furthering the Executive's Vision

In both the public and private sectors, Rumsfeld believed in the importance of having an executive pick key subordinates who will most reliably and effectively further his or her vision for the organization. People are, in his view, the "ribcage of the organization." An executive with a vision will see that the construction of this ribcage is among his or her most important responsibilities. The executive will devote whatever time is necessary to choose the right subordinates to carry out the policy that is to be implemented.

Rumsfeld laid out his vision for DoD fairly clearly in written testimony prior to his second confirmation as Secretary of Defense. In this testimony, he noted, "If confirmed as Secretary, I plan to pursue five key objectives and implement policies and allocate resources needed to achieve those objectives," and he described his five objectives thus:

> First, we need to fashion and sustain deterrence appropriate to the contemporary security environment—a new national security environment. . . .
>
> Second, the readiness and sustainability of deployed forces must be assured. . . .
>
> Third, U.S. command-control-communication, intelligence and space capabilities must be modernized to support 21st Century needs. . . .
>
> Fourth, the U.S. defense establishment must be transformed to address 21st Century circumstances . . . .
>
> Fifth, [we must consider] reform of DOD structures, processes, and organization. (Rumsfeld, 2001)

Rumsfeld gave additional substance to these objectives during the course of the 2001 Quadrennial Defense Review. The final report of the review (found at U.S. Department of Defense, 2001) highlights each of these themes in considerable detail. Rumsfeld realized that working toward his vision would require contributions from all levels of the defense establishment and that his chances of getting those contributions would be maximized if he installed like-minded leaders at key points in the establishment.

Understanding People *and* the Positions to Which They Will Be Assigned

Finding the right people requires understanding the unique demands of various positions at particular points in time. For example, a combatant command engaged in hostilities may require a different kind of leadership than the same command during peacetime. The differences can be seen in comparing the position requirements of U.S. European Command, which now encompasses an area largely at peace but was once at the center of potential conflict between the North Atlantic Treaty Organization and the Warsaw Pact, with those of U.S. Central Command, which encompasses the wars in Afghanistan and Iraq and an overall area that is often in turmoil. Similarly, the required competencies for a given position can change, since the context of a given position has an important bearing on the qualifications demanded of the person who does the job. Finding and recruiting capable candidates and evaluating and developing their potential should be done with full appreciation of the expected context.

Limits on Delegating Responsibilities

Rumsfeld believed that executives can and often must delegate parts of the information-gathering process but that they should not delegate selection decisions for key positions. He believed that executives must invest time and attention in gathering, absorbing, weighing, and acting on information related to these selections. One approach he followed was to ask the military chiefs to identify serving flag/general officers with high potential so that he could seek opportunities to meet and talk with them individually, usually prior to their consideration for any specific position.[8] This expanded his awareness of the available pool.

---

[8] Working through his senior military assistant, Rumsfeld actively sought opportunities to meet with promising leaders during his travels. The appointments would be set up as get-to-know-you sessions and would target officers who had been identified by the military chiefs or who had been suggested to Holcomb, a retired vice admiral who became Rumsfeld's special assistant.

He encouraged those on whom he depended for advice—the Deputy Secretary of Defense, the Chairman of the Joint Chiefs of Staff, and the Vice Chairman of the Joint Chiefs of Staff—to do so as well. This active outreach gave him and his advisers more context for the specific near- and long-term decisions they were to make.

In the end, however, Rumsfeld felt he had a personal responsibility to know as much about the officers he was to recommend to the President as he could. This was not a responsibility he was willing to delegate.

Avoiding Cronyism

Without a robust process, Rumsfeld believed, the tendency is to pick those you know and to overlook better, lesser-known candidates. Clearly, if the best candidates are not picked because they are not known, the organization will not realize its full potential. Additionally, if the pattern of selections seems to consistently favor those who are closest to the executive, others, believing their chances of promotion are lower, leave the organization and thereby diminish the overall quality of the pool. He stressed that the executive needs to be particularly conscious of this potential pitfall because the natural tendency is to be attracted to those with experiences and backgrounds similar to one's own. He was conscious of this in his own experience and saw it being repeated in the military promotion and assignment system.

In this vein, Rumsfeld recounted his experience in his search to fill a key position at G.D. Searle & Company, where he served as chief executive officer and then as president. He employed a search firm, which suggested three candidates. The best candidate from within this group was a friend of Rumsfeld's from college. To guard against his own tendency to hire the familiar rather than the best, he asked for three more candidates and for input from his board of trustees (and others). In the end, he concluded that the friend from college was indeed the best candidate. He hired him, but he did not do so lightly.

Senior Subordinate Participation

The chief executive needs the help of senior subordinates to pinpoint job requirements and find and develop the right people for key positions. He or she also needs advice from key subordinates on promotions and assignments. This advice needs to be offered in private or in a small group setting, and it needs to be specific. But the decisions themselves cannot be delegated, and there is no substitute for the executive's personal involvement in the process. If the chief executive is not willing to devote time and energy to the effort, the key subordinates are less likely to do so. If, on the other hand, the chief executive pays attention to these matters and invests time in these processes, so too will the key subordinates.

Rumsfeld believed his request that the military chiefs periodically brief him on the development and utilization of their flag/general officers served to deepen the chiefs' understanding of their own resources. They knew Rumsfeld would question them about their people, and this compelled them to invest the time necessary to know the answers. In consequence, both Rumsfeld and the military chiefs made better-informed decisions.

Constitutional Principles and Statutory Requirements

The Constitution of the United States establishes the President as the "Commander-in-Chief of the Army and Navy of the United States." The principle of civilian control is embedded in a chain of command that passes through the Secretary of Defense. The chain of command was last modified and clarified by the Goldwater-Nichols Defense Reorganization Act of 1986, which specifies that the chain of command runs directly from the Secretary of Defense to the combatant commanders rather than through the military chiefs.

Consistent with this chain of command, current law (10 U.S.C. 601) requires that officers serving in three- and four-star positions must be appointed by the President with the advice and consent of the Senate. The law further specifies that the Secretary of Defense must inform the President of the qualifications needed in each vacancy and must also submit to the President the Chairman of the Joint Chiefs of Staff's evaluation of the recommended officer's performance in joint assignments. In the lower grades, Senate confirmation is required only upon promotion; however, three- and four-star status must be reconfirmed by the Senate upon any change in position or upon any significant change in the duties associated with a position.

For four-star vacancies in joint positions, there are additional provisions (10 U.S.C. 604) that require each service to submit at least one nominee for consideration by the Secretary of Defense and that allow the Chairman of the Joint Chiefs of Staff to submit other nominees. According to those provisions, the Chairman's evaluation of each nominee "shall primarily consider the performance of the officer as a member of the Joint Staff and in other joint duty assignments, but may include consideration of other aspects of the officer's performance as the Chairman considers appropriate."

Some critics of Rumsfeld's active role in succession management have viewed it as an unwarranted intrusion into the affairs of the Chairman (for joint positions) or the military chiefs (for service positions). But the constitutional and statutory provisions outlined here make it clear that an active role in the appointment of senior military officers is not just an inherent but also a specifically enumerated responsibility of the Secretary of Defense.

Implementation in the Department of Defense

We have observed that the military services tend to optimize succession planning for their own needs but that they do not have responsibility for optimizing succession planning for the whole of DoD. We have also argued that top-level executive engagement is needed to make the succession planning process work. An issue, then, is which senior executive should be held accountable for department-wide senior leader development and utilization.

The Chairman of the Joint Chiefs of Staff can and does play an important role here but needs to remain mindful that he too has been influenced by his own service culture and beliefs. Moreover, the Chairman is responsible for providing military advice to the President and Secretary of Defense but is not responsible for all functions of DoD, some of which benefit from military leadership that is outside the purview of the Chairman's responsibilities. For example, senior officers often perform essential functions on the Secretary of Defense's staff, in defense agencies, or as members of the staffs of the President or other cabinet members. Determining the needs of these positions and the best fit of candidates for these positions may go beyond the responsibilities of the Chairman.

If senior leader development and utilization across DoD is to be optimized, continuous and attentive engagement by the Secretary of Defense—or, at a minimum, the Deputy Secretary of Defense—is needed. These senior executives' engagement can and should be facilitated by staff dedicated to the purpose and by the use of approaches (major ones are recommended later in this monograph) that help to clarify the Secretary's options. The most important decisions, however, should be made personally by those who are most accountable for DoD's short- and long-term performance.

CHAPTER THREE

A Historical View

The Situation When Rumsfeld Assumed Office

When Rumsfeld returned to DoD in January 2001, the environment was right for changing the process for selecting senior leaders. Consistent with the priorities of President George W. Bush, one of Rumsfeld's primary emphases was to "transform" DoD from what he considered to be an industrial-age organization to one that embraced the full potential of information-age capabilities and processes.[1] However, Rumsfeld was unsure, especially in the case of service leadership, that officers chosen by the current leadership—and, potentially, in the image of the current leadership—were best suited to question the status quo and lead a major transformation effort. Indeed, the transformation that Rumsfeld sought to motivate within DoD emphasized jointness—how the military services need to work together to contend with common problems. Rumsfeld viewed DoD as a relatively centrifugal institution: When the services were left to themselves, they tended to pull apart from one another to operate independently. Additionally, he perceived that service leaders had a tendency to dissociate themselves from the issues of other services. He observed that the military chiefs tended not to challenge one another's recommendations for senior leadership positions, even joint positions. Instead, they seemed to endorse a turn-

---

[1] See for example, the following extract from a speech by Bush (1999): "And, if elected, I will set three goals: I will renew the bond of trust between the American president and the American military. I will defend the American people against missiles and terror. And I will begin creating the military of the next century."

taking system that predictably filled senior positions with officers representing the service whose "turn" had arrived. Additionally, Rumsfeld perceived the military leadership to be extremely respectful of, and even deferential to, the community of retired military leaders and thus even more unlikely to challenge the status quo.

Perceived Shortcomings in the Senior Officer Selection Process

Rumsfeld perceived several shortcomings in the selection process that precluded identifying the best candidates for a new DoD leadership. First, he found a lack of explicit consideration both of the qualifications needed in senior positions and of how those qualifications might have evolved or might yet evolve. The existing general/flag officer position descriptions were standard position descriptions, with little variation, that had not been reviewed or revised in the recent past. Clearly the outdated descriptions did not fully or appropriately describe the skills or experience needed by senior leaders who would successfully transform DoD. The descriptions also failed to capture how the positions themselves had changed over time. For example, relative to U.S. European Command or U.S. Southern Command, U.S. Central Command clearly had the greatest potential to become a warfighting command, yet it was not apparent that the demands of the positions were fully captured in the descriptions associated with them.

Further, he found that, although the law requires each of the services to submit at least one recommended nominee for each joint four-star vacancy, he was not always receiving valid or viable recommendations. Instead, he perceived that the system was being manipulated, with one service recommending one strong candidate while the others recommended weaker ones in order to ensure that the services filled positions when it was "their turn" or when it was a position that had traditionally been filled by a particular service.

These shortcomings suggested, overall, a lack of diligence in determining the best candidates for senior military positions. Therefore, because Rumsfeld brought to his position a strong belief that senior executive selection might be one of the most important aspects of his role, change to the process became inevitable. Rumsfeld had long believed that people were the most critical part of an organization and that a leader should select capable people and help them to understand that selecting their subordinates might be the most critical of their duties. However, what Rumsfeld personally lacked upon his return to DoD was a robust knowledge of the existing military leadership. He had last served in DoD as Secretary of Defense from November 1975 to January 1977. Thus, when he returned to DoD in January 2001, he encountered military chiefs who had been only junior field-grade officers during his last tenure as Secretary. As a result, although Rumsfeld recognized the imperative to become more involved in the selection of senior leadership, he initially lacked both deep knowledge of the key players and a process for becoming more involved.

The Introduction and Evolution of a New Process

Overall, Rumsfeld's concerns about the existing senior selection process included the lack of explicit criteria for the positions he was to fill, the fact that the services did not appear to be proposing strong candidates from which to choose, and his lack of knowledge of the bench of senior officers. Nonetheless, the urgency of important assignment decisions confronted him early in his tenure. Just weeks after he assumed his new duties, assignments for two of the combatant commands surfaced for action. Some of the candidates suggested for these positions were also likely candidates for Chairman of the Joint Chiefs of Staff. General Hugh Shelton's assignment as Chairman was scheduled to end in September 2001, and Rumsfeld needed to select a replacement for nomination. Further, the lack of a decision about these top positions was hindering decisions about the assignments for other key senior leader positions: Until the combatant command and Chairman selections were made, it would be difficult to select officers for other senior positions. Yet, Rumsfeld's concerns about the senior officer selection and assignment process were delaying decisions.

Part of the reason for the delay was the time Rumsfeld chose to invest in developing criteria for the Chairman position. Despite its prominence and importance, there was no current and comprehensive description of the responsibilities of the position or of the individual characteristics required to fill it. Rumsfeld and his key participants in the senior leader assignment process developed and then iterated upon the position requirements for the next Chairman. The ten requirements they developed were, as of April 21, 2002,

- capacity for providing the best possible military advice to the National Command Authorities
- broad operational background and experience in major contingencies, including combat and senior command overseas
- a strong, wide-ranging intellect; broad geographic grasp; and experience and understanding of "Washington" beyond things strictly military
- ability to lead—intellectually and managerially—the most senior military officers in support of the administration's proposed strategic changes and transformation agenda
- practical experience in the differing roles of the service chiefs of staff, commanders in chief, and the Joint Staff
- candor and forthrightness—and willingness to disagree—in private counsel to the President and the Secretary of Defense; capacity to exert effective support and leadership once National Command Authority decisions are made
- sufficient credibility with the public and Congress to be convincing in times of crises
- a strong sense of ethics and trustworthiness
- agreement with the administration's views on civilian control
- compatibility with the President, the Vice President, and the Secretary of Defense.[2]

---

[2]   As reported in documentation provided to the authors during research.

Position requirements were also used, at least early in Rumsfeld's tenure, to evaluate candidates against a specific set of criteria.[3] Candidates were also evaluated against broader characteristics that were not position-specific, as shown by evaluation forms (see Figures 3.1 and 3.2) used at different times. Some form entries were marked with an X, and others were filled with letter grades reflecting, for example, the candidates' academic credentials or intellectual capability. The forms also conveyed a summary of evaluations by other senior personnel. Some candidates were cognizant of the evaluation criteria and the matrixes. One combatant commander reported,

> I had three days notice. I interviewed with 17 people. I also had a written test and a personal interview with Rumsfeld. There was a matrix that they used to evaluate candidates, and they used it on me. [They each] filled out a matrix and turned it in to Rumsfeld.

Process Participants

Senior officer selection discussions took place primarily among four key participants, the members of the personnel committee. The committee consisted of the Secretary of Defense, the Deputy Secretary of Defense, the Chairman of the Joint Chiefs of Staff, and the Vice Chairman of the Joint Chiefs of Staff. Rumsfeld recruited Holcomb to facilitate these discussions and the overall senior officer selection process. Although present in Washington only on a part-time basis, Holcomb administered the process, gathered information, and pushed the committee members to make important decisions. Prior to the committee sessions, Holcomb briefed each of the four participants on which decisions were to be made, and he began each committee meeting by describing the candidates being considered in that specific session. Although the final decision was made by Rumsfeld, the participants we interviewed emphasized the free exchange that characterized these sessions and the informal practice of giving each participant an oppor-

---

[3] Formal assessments of individuals were less frequent later during Rumsfeld's tenure. This was because Rumsfeld and the rest of the personnel committee gained greater familiarity with the high-potential candidates. Quantitative evaluations may be most useful when assessing less well-known candidates.

Figure 3.1
Evaluation Form, Earlier Version

POSITION:		
CANDIDATE:	CURRENT POSITION:	
BRIEF BIOGRAPHY:		

SPECIFIC CONSIDERATIONS, THIS ASSIGNMENT

GENERAL CONSIDERATIONS

INNOVATION				OPERATIONAL BACKGROUND		GEOGRAPHICAL EXPERIENCE					JOINT DUTY		UNIQUE QUALIFICATIONS		
R&D	COMMAND	EXERCISE EXPERIENCE	PUBLICATION	COMBAT	CONTINGENCY	PACIFIC	EUROPE	CENTRAL	DC	OTHER	STAFF	OPERATIONS	LANGUAGE	EXCHANGE TOUR	ACADEMIC

VETTING	CHANGE AGENT	ETHICS	CANDOR
DEPSECDEF			
CJCS			
VCJCS			
SERVICE SECRETARY			
SERVICE CHIEF			
USD (POLICY)			
OTHER			

SOURCE: Provided to the authors by OSD personnel.

RAND MG1081-3.1

Figure 3.2
Evaluation Form, Later Version

| CANDIDATE: | INTERVIEWER: |
| CURRENT POSITION: | DATE: |

CHARACTERISTICS CHECK:

| | MILITARY ADVISOR | OPERATIONAL BACKGROUND | | | INTELLECT | BREADTH | | | | ABILITY TO LEAD | DIFFERING ROLES | | |
| | | CONTI-GENCY | CINC | COMBAT | | GEOGRAPHICAL | | | | | OWN SERVICE | JOINT SERVICE | POL. MIL. |
						PACIFIC	EUROPE	DC					
SECDEF													
DEPSECDEF													
CJCS													
VCJCS													
SVC SEC													
SVC CHIEF													
USD (POLICY)													
OTHER													

SOURCE: Provided to the authors by OSD personnel.

RAND MG1081-3.2

tunity to veto the selection. Rumsfeld noted that, in several instances, his initial view of which individual best fit a position changed as a result of the give and take that occurred during the committee discussions. Others expressed agreement with this recollection.

The Introduction of a Key Planning Tool: The Board

The brief period of decision stagnancy at the advent of Rumsfeld's second tenure prompted the creation of one of the key tools of the Rumsfeld assignment process: "the Board," a tactile visual aid. The Board was a large (it was approximately 4 feet tall by 6 feet wide), felt-covered board with movable cards that adhered to the surface. White cards represented each of the most important four-star positions, including joint four-star positions, military chiefs, and vice chiefs. The names of individual officers currently filling those assignments were printed on cards whose color indicated their service and thus permitted users to quickly assess service balance among these positions.[4] The Board was first used to indicate to Rumsfeld the urgency of the pending assignment decisions by visually demonstrating the number of projected vacancies without identified replacements. The board not only served this purpose, spurring steady action following the naming of General Richard Myers to be the next Chairman of the Joint Chiefs of Staff, but also became an integral part of the assignment process discussions among members of the personnel committee.

The photograph of the Board presented in Figure 3.3 shows a snapshot in time. The incumbent names (placed below the position labels) and the selectee names (placed horizontally above the position labels) are mostly legible in this photograph, but we have deliberately obscured the names of candidates being considered for the positions (placed diagonally above the position labels). We have also obscured the names of high-potential candidates being considered, which were placed along the right side of the Board.

---

[4] Service balance was an accepted metric. Although Rumsfeld did pay attention to the balance, he considered it a lesser criterion. He was willing to challenge service balance and unwilling to accept less-qualified candidates solely to maintain service balance.

Figure 3.3
The Board

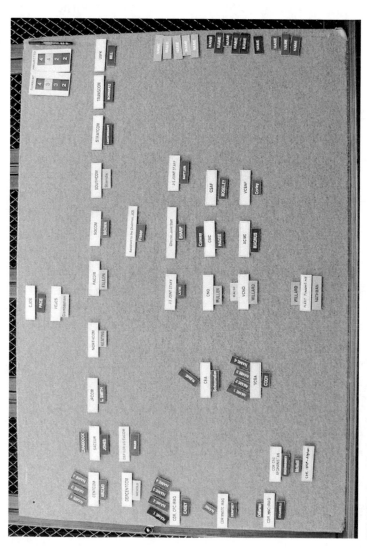

SOURCE: Provided to the authors by OSD personnel.

RAND MG1081-3.3

During discussions, one or more members of the personnel committee often walked to the Board to demonstrate different combinations of personnel changes, showing, for example, how moving officer A to position C allowed for the assignment of another highly capable officer to position B. The Board also allowed the participants to recall who was being held in reserve for future assignments. All of the participants noted that the Board allowed Rumsfeld and his key advisers to focus on the whole of the assignment process, not just its parts.[5]

Two Related Processes

There were two important aspects of the senior officer selection and assignment process: *slating* and *laydowns*. Slating addressed the selection of the best candidates for particular positions and concluded with decisions about who would be recommended to fill specific vacancies. This was the discussion supported, in the case of the most prominent four-star assignments, by the Board.

When Rumsfeld took office in 2001, the process for selecting senior military officers for joint assignments left little to his discretion. The slate of available candidates was determined largely by whom the services chose to recommend, although the Chairman would occasionally add a name to the slate. The names that emerged from this process were first checked within DoD for what is termed *adverse and reportable information* to ensure the candidates were suitable for nomination and confirmation.[6] The Chairman selected a recommended candidate, and his staff prepared a package for the Secretary of Defense's signature that supported the nomination of that candidate. The nomination

---

[5] The Board was kept in Holcomb's office in the Pentagon and, when needed, moved to Rumsfeld's office while covered with a black veil. The staff responsible for moving the Board note that they received long stares from Pentagon staff as they carried the veil-covered board from office to office in preparation for the personnel committee discussions. Great care was taken to keep the contents of the Board hidden from the view of those not directly involved in the personnel discussions. Holcomb photographed the Board after each meeting as a way of recording the discussion.

[6] This screening process actually began before the military services recommended an officer for assignment, and it continued until nomination.

package was then forwarded to the White House for nomination by the President.

As one would expect, given his perspectives on senior leader selection, Rumsfeld was unhappy with his circumscribed role in this process and soon began to change it. He assembled the staff and the processes that allowed him to identify his own candidates in addition to those recommended by the military chiefs and to make informed decisions in his recommendations to the President. Some military chiefs viewed Rumsfeld's and his staff's consideration of candidates the services had not put forward as an unwarranted usurpation of the military chiefs' management prerogatives. Rumsfeld saw it as necessary to finding the best candidates, particularly because some military chiefs, appointed prior to his tenure, might not have shared his vision.

The second process of note was the development and consideration of laydowns. Laydowns were to be developed within each service by the civilian service secretary and the military chief of staff. Some were actually developed by the military chief, and others were developed by supporting staff. The laydown discussion between each military chief and Rumsfeld typically included consideration of prospective candidates for a variety of future positions, sometimes more than one rotation into the future. Laydowns also included a review of the qualifications of senior general/flag officers and rising junior general/ flag officers with high potential. For each officer reviewed in the laydown, the service chief provided a summary of qualifications and key experiences and recommended a series of assignments leading to the expected pinnacle assignment of that officer's career.

In prior administrations, most of the consideration and deliberation related to officer development had generally been left to the individual services. However, Rumsfeld included this second aspect in his senior officer selection and assignment process, as he wanted to understand the bench of future leaders.

Understanding how the services develop future leaders is not just a good practice for the Secretary of Defense to follow; knowing the bench also supported Rumsfeld's process in several other important ways. First, it allowed Rumsfeld and other members of the personnel committee to meet officers who had been identified by their service as likely candidates for future opportunities. While traveling, Rumsfeld scheduled meetings with these general/flag officers and used these purposeful interactions to develop impressions of officers, many of whom likely did not know that they had been "interviewed." When the services provided their laydowns, they also provided Rumsfeld with an understanding of, and an opportunity to influence, both how officers were being developed and which types of assignments were prioritized as developmental opportunities. Further, this accumulated knowledge of the service benches also supported the slating discussions within the personnel committee: If Rumsfeld and other members of the personnel committee had deep knowledge of the services' laydowns, the services need not be involved as deeply in the slating discussions.

However, the laydown aspect of senior leader selection was new to most of the services. Although Rumsfeld requested that the military chiefs meet individually with him twice a year to discuss laydowns, not all of the military chiefs did so or saw the value in such interactions. Some of the chiefs believed the laydown discussions were less important than the slating discussions and final decisions, from which they felt largely excluded. This was especially true in the case of the services that had not traditionally managed their officers beyond the next assignment cycle; thinking about long-term development of senior leaders was a new challenge for those services. From Rumsfeld's perspective, however, laydown discussions provided a chance to gain an overall perspective on the promising candidates from each of the services. If laydowns were crafted and presented well, the service's input to the slating for specific assignments would be apparent. Further, Rumsfeld felt that the chiefs should be able to answer questions about the potential and development of individual officers, including why an individual was or was not a strong candidate for future opportunities. However, some of the military chiefs appeared to have difficulty crafting a concise and targeted laydown briefing and answering questions about individual officers.

One service that had been managing senior leaders with a long-term perspective shared with Rumsfeld its approach to crafting potential assignment paths for individual officers. This approach included a candid assessment of an individual's strengths and weaknesses. In many cases, those weaknesses were addressed through a developmental plan that, for example, provided an officer deficient in certain expertise with the needed political/military or regional experience. In other instances, weaknesses pertaining to the officer's style or other personal capabilities either limited the choice of assignments for that officer or decreased the likelihood of future assignments altogether. Rumsfeld was sufficiently impressed with this approach that he encouraged the other services to model their materials after this particular service's "book." Service representatives recounted their efforts to replicate the presentation material. However, they do not appear to have realized that that it was more than the presentation that Rumsfeld valued: It was the entire long-term perspective, which included a candid assessment of both strengths and weaknesses, that Rumsfeld considered important.

The Prioritization of Assignments

Rumsfeld actively assessed the priority of different assignments. This assessment was largely enabled by the Board, which afforded users an understanding of the overall assignment slate being developed. In general, after the attacks of September 11, 2001, Rumsfeld perceived joint, and especially warfighting, positions as the most important assignments. Further, he placed a new and different emphasis on the deputy commander positions at the combatant commands. Those positions had previously been filled with senior, experienced officers in their pinnacle assignment, and these officers typically retired after holding these positions. However, Rumsfeld felt it important to consider these positions as developmental assignments and to give them to officers who were likely to continue to serve in other assignments. Their job as the deputy was, in part, to prepare to be the commander at that particular command or at another command. This was a very different perspective on these joint assignments.

Similarly, when filling senior joint assignments, Rumsfeld was typically less supportive of the selection of officers who had not already accumulated significant joint experience. Not surprisingly, given these emphases, Rumsfeld was interested in assignments to all joint positions, not just the most senior ones. For example, Rumsfeld and his advisers noted that two- or three-star officers assigned field commands in Iraq or Afghanistan would have considerable influence on carrying out policy direction; that is, their influence would extend well beyond the tactical direction of troops in the field. Their decisions would not only be a reflection of policy but ultimately would establish policy in key areas.[7] Rumsfeld and his advisers thought it important that they have a voice in the screening and selection of these officers.

The process implemented during Rumsfeld's tenure focused on all three- and four-star positions, but, with additional time as Secretary, Rumsfeld would have extended the senior leader assignment process to include joint one- and two-star positions as well.

Who Gets to Choose?

Much of the discussion about the Rumsfeld process for senior officer selection tended to focus on perceptions of his interactions with the military chiefs. Most of the military chiefs felt that the selection of senior officers was rightfully their role and that only the approval and administration of the nomination belonged to the Secretary of Defense. Although prior Secretaries of Defense had occasionally intervened in the selection of senior officers, they had tended to focus on key joint positions and chiefs of service and not to be involved in decisions about service positions or three-star positions. To the extent that there was resistance to an expanded role for the Secretary of Defense, this resistance was sometimes exacerbated by the interaction between Rumsfeld and the military chiefs.

Interviews revealed different perceptions of the interaction among the key players in this process, especially among Rumsfeld and the military chiefs. Although some chiefs believed that Rumsfeld was not receptive to input, others underscored his receptiveness to alternatives. Several individuals reported that they felt that they could challenge any of Rumsfeld's decisions and that Rumsfeld would listen to a different perspective and reconsider his initial decision. The interactions

---

[7]   For example, instruction and oversight regarding the treatment of prisoners in Iraq became a major issue of policy debate. The senior military officer in Iraq had primary responsibility for setting policy in this area.

between the different military chiefs and Rumsfeld appear to have varied for several reasons. First, Rumsfeld preferred relatively simple presentations, and this preference was difficult to accommodate given DoD culture, which favored complex slide presentations that tended to capture all available information as opposed to the most relevant information.

Second, Rumsfeld was inclined to challenge assertions, especially those regarding the services' candidates. To the extent that his challenging questions were addressed, accounts suggest that Rumsfeld was typically receptive to the answers. One of the military chiefs who others felt interacted especially effectively with Rumsfeld told us that he often assessed, in the first few minutes of a session with Rumsfeld, whether the session was proceeding smoothly, including whether he was able to address the questions Rumsfeld asked. In some instances, if he felt the discussion was not particularly productive, the chief suggested an adjournment after a few minutes. He then rescheduled the meeting for a time when he felt there might be better give and take or for a future date that would afford him sufficient time to adjust his presentation and supplement his own information.

Third, Rumsfeld expected the military chiefs to know their people and to understand the basis for information they provided about the strengths and weaknesses of an officer. He also wanted the chiefs to demonstrate that they were relying on more than their own opinion or experience when offering views on their leadership bench. He wanted to know what process and criteria had been used to develop the recommendations that were being offered.[8] If a military chief presented a list of candidates and was not able to explain why some officers had been characterized in certain ways, the chief was likely to face more-challenging questions from Rumsfeld. Thus, military chiefs who relied most heavily on others to manage their general/flag officers or who presented the most complex information were most likely to experience challenging sessions with the Secretary of Defense. One participant in the process noted that chiefs who were most frustrated with the process

---

[8] One chief noted that "Rumsfeld wanted to be sure that we were not advocating for our cousin or nephew."

had "answers but no logic," whereas Rumsfeld wanted to understand the logic behind the recommendations.

Further, the military chiefs often felt that they were not informed appropriately of the decisions made or the logic behind the decisions. They also were frustrated by the delays in making some key personnel decisions. The lack of information often made it difficult for military chiefs to manage their own organizations and to keep key parties informed of likely actions. During interviews, Rumsfeld and his key aides acknowledged these communication difficulties. Although he was quick to emphasize the importance of the senior leader selection process that he introduced, Rumsfeld also acknowledged that the process took an unfortunate toll, in some instances, on the relationship between the Secretary of Defense and the military leadership.

Changes to the Process After Rumsfeld's Departure

Secretary of Defense Gates assumed his position in December 2006. Aware that the Rumsfeld process had aggravated some of the military chiefs, Gates decided, with General Peter Pace, then–Chairman of the Joint Chiefs of Staff, that the deliberation process for senior leader selection should be returned to the uniformed services, and he relieved Holcomb of his duties. While Pace was Chairman, the services had the largest role in selecting leaders for the three-star positions in their own services. The process for four-star positions and for three-star positions with joint responsibilities was primarily administered by the Joint Chiefs of Staff. Pace led the slating discussions regarding senior leader selection among the chiefs in the chiefs' regular meetings, which were also known as *tank sessions*.[9] Gates participated in the tank sessions approximately once a week, but the bulk of the conversation took place among the military chiefs, the Chairman, and the Vice Chairman. When the Joint Chiefs of Staff arrived at a decision, Pace briefed the outcome to Gates, who typically approved the recommendation.

---

[9]   The *tank* is the secure area in which the Joint Chiefs of Staff hold their meetings. Decisions made "in the tank" are those in which the Joint Chiefs of Staff collectively participate.

The scope of the discussions undertaken at the tank sessions was an important change relative to Rumsfeld's process. Rumsfeld's process had encompassed all three- and four-star positions, but Gates and Pace chose to focus the process on four-star positions and on a subset of three-star positions (i.e., those that had joint responsibilities, such as joint task force commands, Navy fleet commands, and numbered Air Force commands). They decided to return responsibility for other selections to the military chiefs and to hold the chiefs accountable for their choices. Another important change occurred in the conduct of the laydown discussions. The laydown discussions ceased for a period after Rumsfeld's departure; when later reinstated, the discussions were held between the chiefs and the Chairman.

Mullen, who replaced Pace as Chairman of the Joint Chiefs of Staff in 2007, indicated to the military chiefs that he wanted to know about the most promising one- and two-star officers, and he also informed the combatant commanders that he wanted to know about promising officers serving within their commands. Mullen has also encouraged the military chiefs to present their laydown plans to Gates.

Another important change occurred regarding the extent to which decisions are optimized and alternative selections considered. The current process lacks anything resembling the Board that was prominent in the Rumsfeld process. Although the Board is not the only tool that could facilitate the consideration of multiple candidates for multiple positions, current participants suggest that alternatives are not being fully considered to the extent facilitated by the Board. According to participants, currently, decisions are primarily focused on an eight-month horizon, which is shorter than that considered by Rumsfeld's process, which eventually came to consider one to two moves beyond the current selection (i.e., often three to four years into the future).

There are both critics and proponents of the system that emerged after Rumsfeld's departure. One frequently mentioned positive aspect of the current process is that it is more transparent to the uniformed participants. The military chiefs are not only involved in the primary deliberations but are also informed promptly when the Secretary of Defense has decided to select a particular candidate. Further, they are able to inform the candidates prior to a formal announcement, of the decision. This open aspect of the system has been especially well received by the critics of the Rumsfeld system, which one of the most adamant critics described as a "close-hold, gossip-based parlor game." The closed nature of the Rumsfeld system was perhaps more a reflection of Rumsfeld's decision style than of the system itself. That is, there was nothing inherent in the Rumsfeld system that required it to be open or closed.

CHAPTER FOUR

A Process View

In this chapter, we recapitulate the essential elements of the senior leader management processes before, during, and after Rumsfeld's second tenure as Secretary of Defense. As described in the previous chapter, the process evolved during Rumsfeld's tenure. In this chapter, we describe it as it stood at the time of his departure, in its final state.

In our earlier discussion of succession management concepts, we mentioned that fully developed succession management processes involve both development and utilization elements. Developmental elements focus on identifying future human capital needs; indentifying those with high potential to meet those needs; and investing appropriately in the training, education, and experience of the high-potential candidates. Utilization processes focus on matching the available talent and the immediate needs of the organization. This chapter shows that an essential difference between the Rumsfeld process and those that preceded and followed it is that the Rumsfeld process emphasized the developmental elements and a broader form of utilization considerations that extends beyond filling immediate vacancies one at a time.

Except as noted, our discussion in this chapter is limited to the filling of three- and four-star positions. These require individual presidential nomination and Senate confirmation and thus entail a level of decisionmaking that is far greater than that required for one- and two-star positions.[1]

---

[1] Officers are generally selected for promotion to one- and two-star rank by promotion boards. Such officers hold *rank in person*; that is, their rank moves with them regardless of position. Presidential nomination and Senate confirmation of the promotion lists is required,

The Prior Process

The process inherited by Rumsfeld and his team in 2001 was designed to fill vacancies as they occurred. It began with identifying a future vacancy and then proceeded to soliciting service candidates (for joint positions), selecting a nominee, vetting the nominee, and obtaining Senate confirmation. Figure 4.1 shows the steps in the process for joint positions. For these positions, the process was limited to immediate utilization considerations, with no venue for the consideration of developmental objectives. The process also lacked an optimization element, which would have allowed multiple candidates and multiple expected vacancies to be considered simultaneously in order to maximize the fit of people to positions. Selections were made primarily by the Chairman, who typically consulted with the military chiefs and occasionally with combatant commanders. Some Secretaries of Defense were more involved with the Chairman in selecting candidates, but they typically focused on key four-star positions. For most other positions, the Secretary of Defense received a nomination package that, although it contained all the nominees, was built around the Chairman's selection. Rumsfeld related that he was expected to sign the package he received and that it was not designed to help him weigh other alternatives.

Figure 4.2 depicts the steps for filling positions within the services. Selections were made by the military chief or secretary of the service (or both), and the Secretary of Defense was expected to approve the selection. The Chairman had little or no role in the process, other than filling his statutory responsibility to comment on the joint performance of the nominee. The services had an opportunity to game-plan their selections—that is, to consider both development and utilization needs—and undoubtedly did so, to greater or lesser degrees. Because we are uncertain of the extent or nature of the game-planning done by the services, that step is enclosed in a dashed line.

---

but presidential or Senate action on assignments of these officers to specific positions is not required. However, at the three- and four-star levels, rank is tied to position, and each appointment at that level requires presidential nomination and Senate confirmation.

Figure 4.1
The Prior Process for Senior Joint Position Nominations

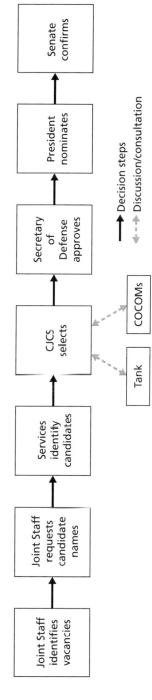

NOTES: CJCS = Chairman of the Joint Chiefs of Staff. COCOM = combatant commander.
RAND MG1081-4.1

Figure 4.2
The Prior Process for Service Position Nominations

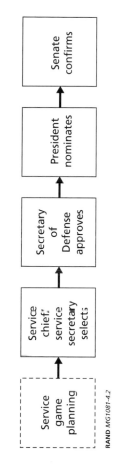

RAND MG1081-4.2

The Evolved Rumsfeld Process

In its final form, the Rumsfeld process contained multiple inputs and decision loops that contrast sharply with the much more linear process Rumsfeld inherited in 2001. Additionally, the process was essentially the same for both joint and service positions at the three- and four-star levels. The process was also used for some one- and two-star positions in key warfighting areas, particularly the U.S. Central Command area of responsibility. Central to this process, depicted in Figure 4.3, was the personnel committee. The committee met once or twice a month to deliberate alternatives.

One point of entry to the process was the identification of vacancies by the Joint Staff or the services. The personnel committee or its supporting staff would then ask the services to recommend candidates, and a special assistant would assemble suggested slates that fit the candidates to the expected vacancies within some time horizon, often with the aid of the slating Board. This process allowed multiple candidates to be considered for multiple positions simultaneously, thereby affording greater optimality in the overall match of people and positions,

Figure 4.3
The Rumsfeld Process

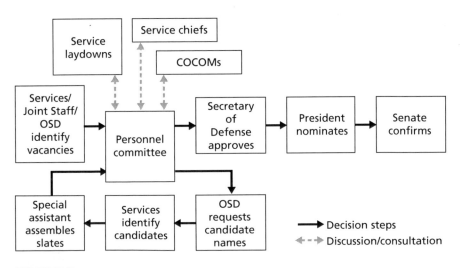

RAND MG1081-4.3

including the distribution of talent to joint and service positions. The suggested slates might include candidates not identified by the services. Names might be added or deleted through the deliberations of the personnel committee. When decisions were finalized, the services were tasked to prepare their formal nomination packages. From that point, the process proceeded through the required formal steps to Senate confirmation.

Another point of entry to the process was the semi-annual laydown, provided to the Secretary by each military chief, of service flag/general officer assessments and recommended assignment paths for high-potential officers. The laydowns informed the Secretary's efforts to gain greater familiarity with high-potential officers. They also conditioned some of the decisions of the personnel committee: The Secretary's agreement with an assignment path during a laydown session could be invoked by a military chief in later slating decisions.

The role of the special assistant was particularly important in the development of slates and the translation of laydown information into specific slating recommendations. The special assistant routinely solicited the views of the chiefs and service secretaries in developing draft slates for consideration by the personnel committee. The special assistant also reflected laydown discussions in the development of future slates. The special assistant's office maintained all key records associated with the process.

The Subsequent Process

After Rumsfeld's departure in 2006, the process for filling joint and service vacancies largely reverted to a linear form that was similar to the one Rumsfeld had inherited in 2001. As shown in Figure 4.4, the subsequent process, still in effect today, differs from the pre-Rumsfeld process in two key respects. First, selection decisions are made in the tank rather than by the Chairman alone. This affords the military chiefs greater participation in the selections than they enjoyed during the pre-Rumsfeld process and the Rumsfeld processes, but it isolates the Secretary from the process. Second, although service laydowns,

Figure 4.4
The Post-Rumsfeld Process for Senior Joint Position Nominations

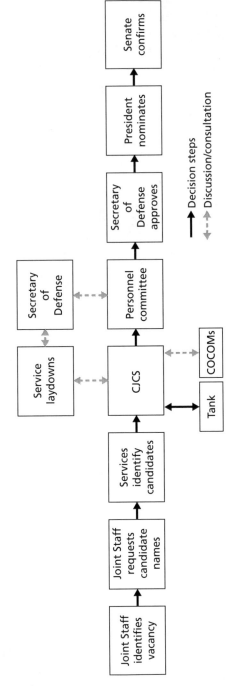

RAND *MG1081-4.4*

which initially were suspended, were reinstated during some periods, the Chairman and the Secretary were addressed in separate sessions. Another important difference from the pre-Rumsfeld process is that, because the current process focuses on one or a few vacancies at a time, optimization tends to be missing.

The process for filling in-service assignments has reverted to the pre-Rumsfeld form. When service laydowns are held, they provide an opportunity for the military chiefs and the Chairman to deconflict plans for service versus joint utilization of some officers. There remains the risk, however, that the military services will husband their best talent for service positions.

Assessing the Processes

Chapter Two describes six elements we found to be important in managing the succession of senior military leaders. The three processes just described can be assessed by observing the degree to which they incorporate these six elements. Table 4.1 summarizes our observations. A black checkmark indicates that the applicable element was robustly implemented in a process. A gray checkmark indicates a more limited implementation of an element. The absence of a checkmark indicates that the element was or is not a consistent feature of the process.

We found that the prior and subsequent processes partially focused on key positions. All of the processes focused on joint positions, but only the Rumsfeld process meaningfully engaged the Secretary and Chairman in decisions about service positions. When service positions are filled through processes that are disconnected from the consideration of joint position demands, the optimal fit of people to assignments is not likely to be achieved. A service's decision to reassign an officer practically removes him or her from the pool of officers available for joint assignments for some period.

Neither the prior nor subsequent processes incorporated an explicit identification of qualifications sought in the position. When the desired qualifications are not made explicit, the process of assessing the candidates for specific positions is likely less structured. In the

Table 4.1
Assessing the Processes

	Prior Process	Rumsfeld Process	Subsequent Process
Focus on key positions	✓	✓	✓
Identify position-specific competency requirements and qualifications		✓	
Identify and assess high-potential candidates	✓	✓	✓
Match pools of candidates and positions, considering both near- and long-term successions		✓	✓
Use career paths to deepen and widen candidate pools		✓	✓
Engage senior executives in the process	✓	✓	✓

Rumsfeld process, there were early efforts to build templates that identified desired position qualifications, but there is no indication that use of the templates persisted in later selections. Thus, in the Rumsfeld process, there was limited implementation of this element.

Outside of the Rumsfeld process, we saw no evidence of centralized, systematic identification, assessment, and development of high-potential candidates for future vacancies in senior joint positions. Some service-centric efforts, however, almost certainly occurred.

In the prior and subsequent processes, vacancies appear to have been or to be considered one or a few at a time. Simultaneously considering multiple candidates for multiple positions affords a better fit of the available inventory and allows for balancing immediate utilization and long-term development needs.

Service laydowns, combined with a pooled approach to matching people and positions, created a strong potential in the Rumsfeld process to use career paths for development purposes. The subsequent process incorporates laydowns, but its apparent one-at-a-time approach to filling vacancies lessens the likelihood that developmental considerations will influence selections.

The concept of using a committee to deliberate on selection recommendations was carried over from the Rumsfeld process to the subsequent process. This means that the current Secretary is likely involved in the process to a greater extent than predecessors who participated in the prior process. However, it is the Chairman rather than the Secretary who is the key source of advice and who is hence the decision-maker in the subsequent process. Consequently, the "ribcage of the organization" has a strong potential to reflect the Chairman's vision more so than the Secretary's.

Overall, we found the Rumsfeld process, as it finally evolved, to contain all of the expected elements of a fully formed succession management system. As implemented, however, it was not without its detractors. The primary complaint of key stakeholders (mainly, the military chiefs) was lack of transparency. They were excluded from the deliberations of the personnel committee. Some of them did not fully understand the role of the special assistant who managed the process for the Secretary or how they were expected to interact with him. Some were uncomfortable with the laydown process and did not comprehend how it could shape subsequent assignment decisions.

The chiefs' concerns about lack of transparency were likely exacerbated by Rumsfeld's practice of considering candidates other than those they had identified. This practice meant that a decision made by the personnel committee could disrupt a service chief's plans using a specific officer. It also implied that consideration for joint assignments took precedence over consideration for service assignments. Perhaps the chiefs' concerns would have been allayed if, prior to holding personnel committee sessions, Rumsfeld and his special assistant had been more forthcoming with the military chiefs regarding who was being considered for what position. Extensive precoordination of all alternatives with the military chiefs would likely have dampened the spontaneity that was a useful feature of the personnel committee deliberations. But some middle course, such as Rumsfeld empowering his special assistant to periodically consult with the military chiefs regarding ongoing deliberations, might have improved the process. The military chiefs, in turn, might have provided additional information on emerging candidates that was unknown to Rumsfeld and his staff. We therefore consider engagement of senior executives to have been implemented in a limited fashion in the Rumsfeld process.

Another concern interviewees expressed with the Rumsfeld process was that it consumed a significant portion of the Secretary's time. By some estimates, Rumsfeld devoted about 20 percent of his time to succession management tasks. Rumsfeld himself, however, felt that this cost was proportional to its benefit. Others occupying the Secretary's office may have a different sense of how their time should be allocated. Within a robust process, there is undoubtedly room for variation in details, such as how much of the information gathering is delegated, how much optimization is done by staff rather than the principals, how much structure is built into the decision processes, and how much voice is afforded to key stakeholders (such as military chiefs and combatant commanders). These details can render the process more or less time-consuming for the Secretary. But if the Secretary of Defense does not reserve the right to make key succession management decisions, and if he does not accumulate the information needed to make those decisions insightfully, the Secretary will fail to exploit a major tool that could be used to influence DoD outcomes.

CHAPTER FIVE

Conclusions and Recommendations

Early in his second tenure as Secretary of Defense, Rumsfeld recognized that the process he inherited for selecting military officers for senior positions did not meet his needs. Decisions that he considered critical to transforming his department and shaping its outcomes relied too heavily on the judgments of others and on information perhaps held by others but not by Rumsfeld himself. The process he inherited also violated his sense of the appropriate role for a chief executive, which was based on his extensive experience in both the public and private sectors. He brought on a special assistant, who worked with a small staff, to remake the process. Their approach evolved over a number of years, during which time Rumsfeld and his staff added and refined tools and procedures while expanding the range of key positions addressed by the process.

The most important element injected by Rumsfeld and his team was the active, engaged participation of the Secretary of Defense in selecting officers for senior positions and in identifying and developing lower-ranking officers with the potential to occupy senior positions in the future. Another important element was the simultaneous consideration of multiple candidates for multiple joint and service vacancies, a change that sought a more optimal match of talent and tasks throughout DoD. Both of these elements were introduced during Rumsfeld's second tenure, and both appear to have been significantly deemphasized after his departure.

The process that emerged after Rumsfeld's tenure is directed by the Chairman of the Joint Chiefs of Staff and supported by the General

Officer Management Office (GOMO) under the Director of the Joint Staff. It features some consideration of long-term developmental needs via periodic laydowns briefed by the military chiefs to the Chairman and the Secretary. The military chiefs are comfortable with the process because key joint nominations are discussed in the tank and because the selection of officers for service assignments is left largely to the military chiefs and secretaries. However, there is no evidence of an optimization function in the process. The Secretary's recommendations to the President for appointment to key senior positions are, therefore, largely predetermined through deliberations in which he did not take part and are packaged in increments of one vacancy at a time, which minimizes the system's capacity to find the best fit of people to positions.

To improve the current process, we propose the following recommendations:

- Consider establishing a senior GOMO within OSD, with its chief reporting directly to the Secretary of Defense, to provide staff support for joint succession planning. This office would facilitate decisions for all joint and service three- and four-star positions and for select one- and two-star positions. It could be headed by a retired general/flag officer with extensive joint experience, good personnel and resource management skills, and a well-established reputation for rising above service parochialism. To avoid even the appearance of a conflict of interest, the senior GOMO should have no other responsibilities. If the trusted assistant heading the GOMO were a retired general/flag officer, that individual would best have been retired from active service for at least ten years so as to be reasonably well removed from his or her immediate peer groups. The chief of the senior GOMO would be employed full-time as a member of the senior executive service.
- Require the senior GOMO to develop tools and information systems to support simultaneous consideration of multiple candidates for multiple positions. The senior GOMO would develop alternative plans for filling expected joint and service vacancies, and these plans, in the interest of transparency, would be coordinated individually with military chiefs and combatant command-

ers and collectively in tank sessions with the Joint Chiefs of Staff. The senior GOMO would present alternative plans to the personnel committee (consisting, as before, of the Secretary, Deputy Secretary, Chairman, and Vice Chairman) for its consideration and modification.

- Require the senior GOMO to maintain descriptions of the qualifications and expertise required for senior positions. These position descriptions should be revisited each time the position is filled to ensure both that the qualifications remain accurate and that the selected officer is the best candidate.
- Clarify the purpose and desired content of service laydowns, focusing them specifically on longer-term personnel plans. Laydowns should focus on key senior assignments and only on the officers with the potential to fill them within the next two to four cycles of assignment. (This will restrict consideration to only 10–20 percent of all general/flag officers.) Laydowns should candidly assess both the strengths and the weaknesses of officers, and they should highlight further developmental experience needed to prepare these selected officers for future key roles. The senior GOMO should provide a repository for service laydowns and periodically coordinate with service GOMOs and the Joint Staff GOMO to ensure that high-potential one- and two-star officers are being developed in a manner consistent with the laydowns.
- The Secretary and Deputy Secretary of Defense should be closely involved in the selection of senior leaders and should understand the strengths and weaknesses of each selected officer as well as the characteristics of the candidates not selected for each position. As the traditional overseer of DoD business and management processes, the Deputy Secretary of Defense should have a significant voice in making officer assignments in the case of positions that entail responsibilities in these areas.
- The Secretary of Defense, with the participation of the personnel committee, should explicitly prioritize senior leader positions and ensure that the best candidates are being selected for the highest-priority positions. This will require the simultaneous assessment of multiple positions and assignment opportunities.

References

Bush, George W., "A Period of Consequences," speech at The Citadel, South Carolina, September 23, 1999.

Fulmer, Robert M., and Jay Alden Conger, *Growing Your Company's Leaders: How Great Organizations Use Succession Management to Sustain Competitive Advantage*, New York: Amacom, 2004.

Gabarro, John J., *The Dynamics of Taking Charge*, Boston: Harvard Business School Press, 1987.

Graham, Bradley, "By His Own Rules: The Ambitions, Successes, and Ultimate Failures of Donald Rumsfeld," *Public Affairs*, 2009, pp. 330–331.

Hardy, Lynn, "Self-Leadership as a Tool in Management Succession Planning," *The Public Manager*, Vol. 33, No. 3, Winter 2004–2005, pp. 41–44.

Harrell, Margaret C., Harry J. Thie, Peter Schirmer, and Kevin Brancato, *Aligning the Stars: Improvements to General and Flag Officer Management*, Santa Monica, Calif.: RAND Corporation, MR-1712-OSD, 2004. As of February 22, 2011: http://www.rand.org/pubs/monograph_reports/MR1712.html

Huang, Tung-Chun, "Succession Management Systems and Human Resource Management Outcomes," *International Journal of Manpower*, Vol. 22, No. 8, 2001, pp. 736–747.

Jarrell, Karen M., and Kyle Coby Pewitt, "Succession Planning in Government: Case Study of a Medium-Sized City," *Review of Public Personnel Administration*, Vol. 27, No. 3, September 2007, pp. 297–309.

Lynn, Dahlia Bradshaw, "Succession Management Strategies in Public Sector Organizations," in Montgomery Van Wart and Lisa A. Dicke, eds., *Administrative Leadership in the Public Sector*, Armon, N.Y.: M. E. Sharpe, 2008.

McCall, Morgan W., Jr., *High Flyers: Developing the Next Generation of Leaders*, Boston: Harvard Business School Press, 1998.

McCall, Morgan W., Jr., Michael M. Lombardo, and Ann M. Morrison, *The Lesson of Experience: How Successful Executives Develop on the Job*, New York: The Free Press, 1989.

Morrison, Robert F., and Roger R. Hock, "Career Building: Learning from Cumulative Work Experience," in Douglas T. Hall, ed., *Career Development in Organizations*, San Francisco: Jossey-Bass, 1986.

NAPA—*See* National Academy of Public Administration.

National Academy of Public Administration, *Managing Succession and Developing Leadership: Growing the Next Generation of Public Service Leaders*, Washington, D.C.: National Academy of Public Administration, 1997.

Public Law 99-433, The Goldwater-Nichols Department of Defense Reorganization Act of 1986, October 1, 1986.

Rumsfeld, Donald H., *Statement of the Honorable Donald H. Rumsfeld. Prepared for the Confirmation Hearing Before the U.S. Senate Committee on Armed Services*, January 11, 2001.

United States Code, Title 10, Section 433, Relationship with Other Federal Laws, February 1, 2010.

United States Code, Title 10, Section 601, Positions of Importance and Responsibility: Generals and Lieutenant Generals; Admirals and Vice Admirals, February 1, 2010.

United States Code, Title 10, Section 604, Senior Joint Officer Positions: Recommendations to the Secretary of Defense, February 1, 2010.

U.S. Department of Defense, *Quadrennial Defense Review Report*, Washington, D.C., September 30, 2001.